Evan Hause

Elephant Breath

for Percussion Quartet

ISBN 978-1-4803-4256-9

EDWARD B.
MARKS MUSIC
COMPANY

EXCLUSIVELY DISTRIBUTED BY

HAL•LEONARD®
CORPORATION

7777 W. BLUEMOUND RD. P.O. BOX 13819 MILWAUKEE, WI 53213

www.ebmarks.com
www.halleonard.com

Key to consistent staff usage (with abbreviations):

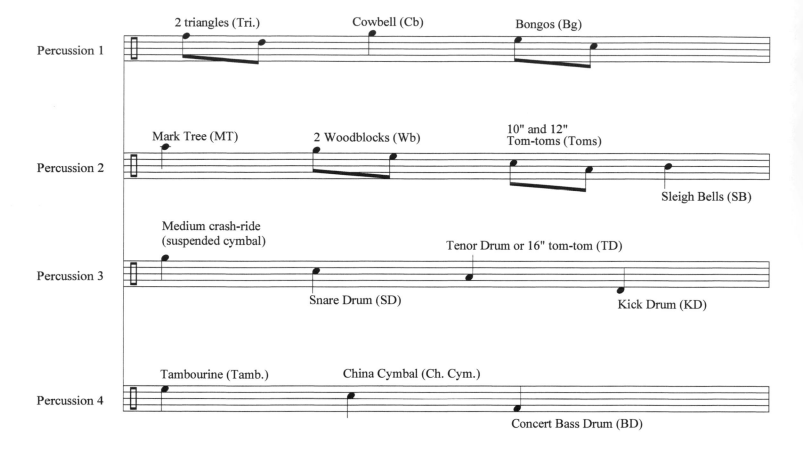

Elephant Breath was composed for and premiered by the Pittsburg State University Percussion Ensemble, under the direction of the Composer, May 6, 1997 in McCray Auditorium, Pittsburg, Kansas.

duration: *ca.* 5'

Cover drawing by William Bolcom

DURATION: *ca.* 5:00

Written for and premiered by the Pittsburg State University Percussion Ensemble, Directed by the Composer, May 6, 1997, McCray Hall, Pittsburg, Kansas

Elephant Breath

Evan Hause
(1997)

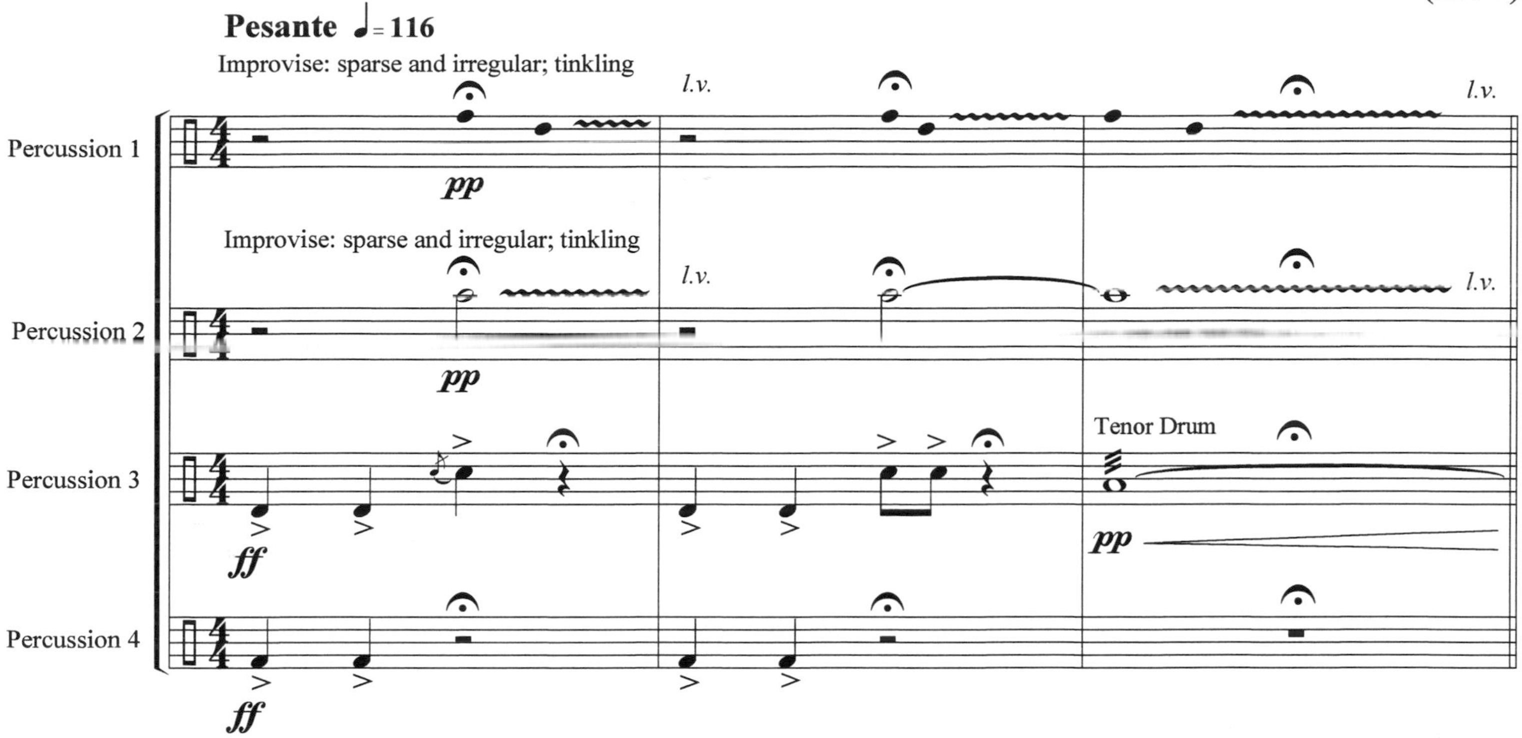

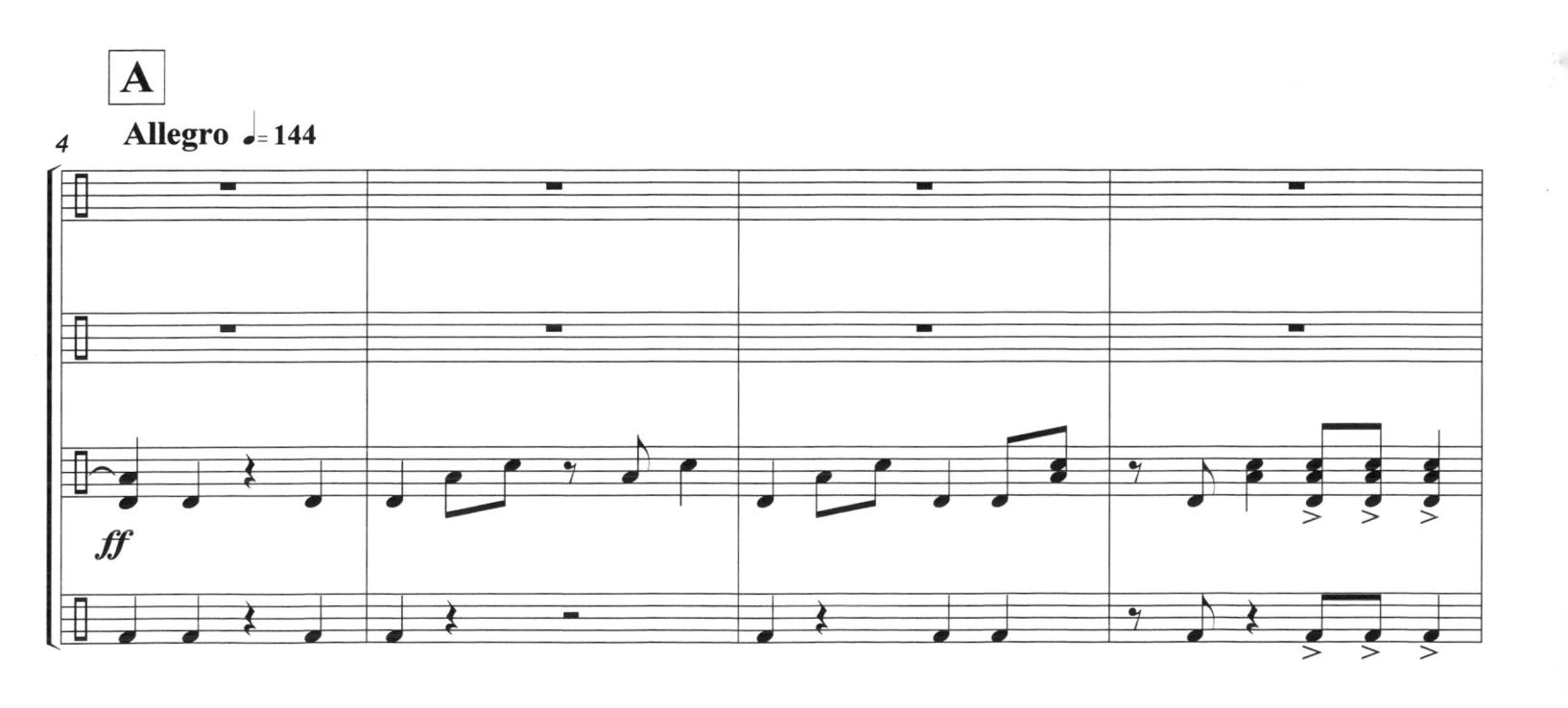

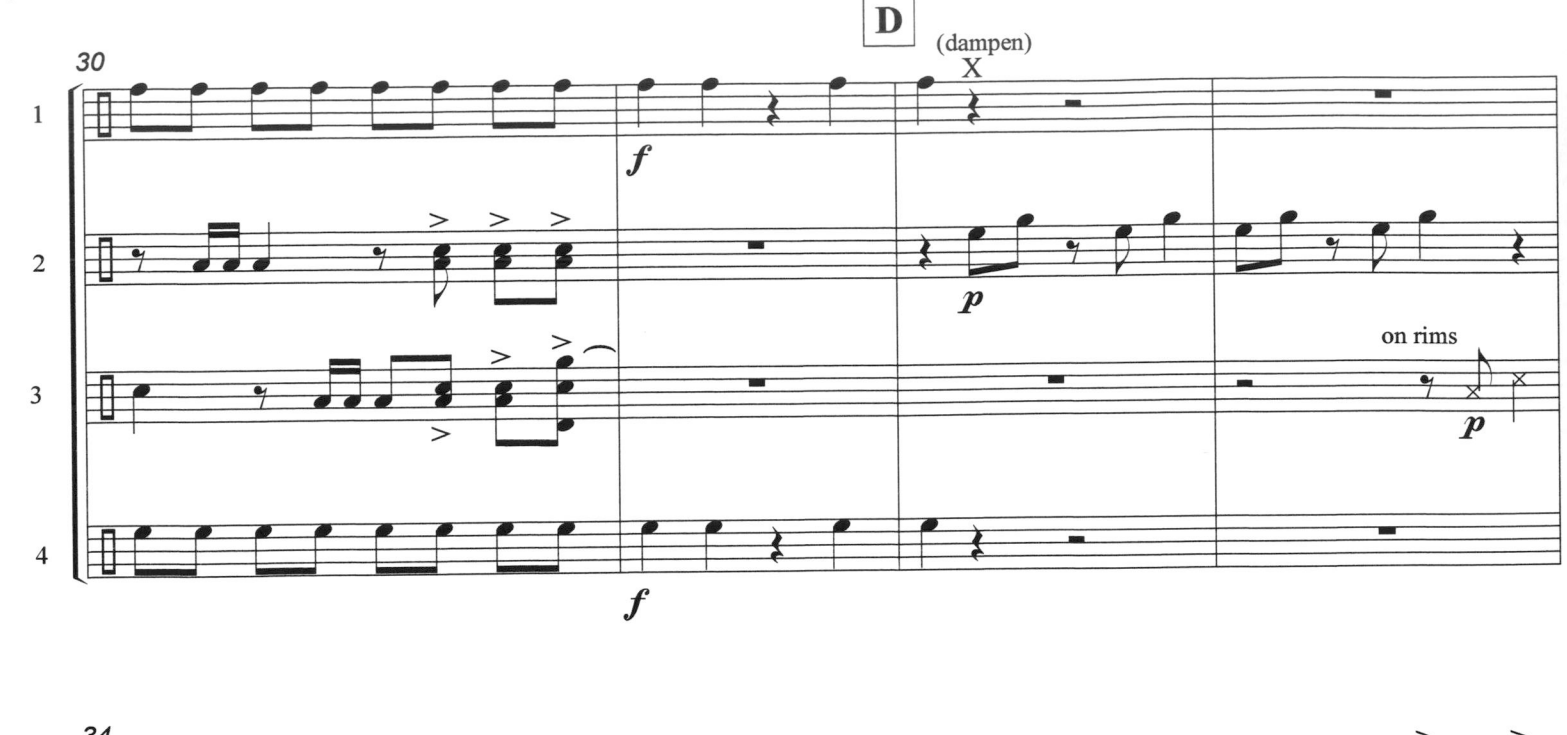

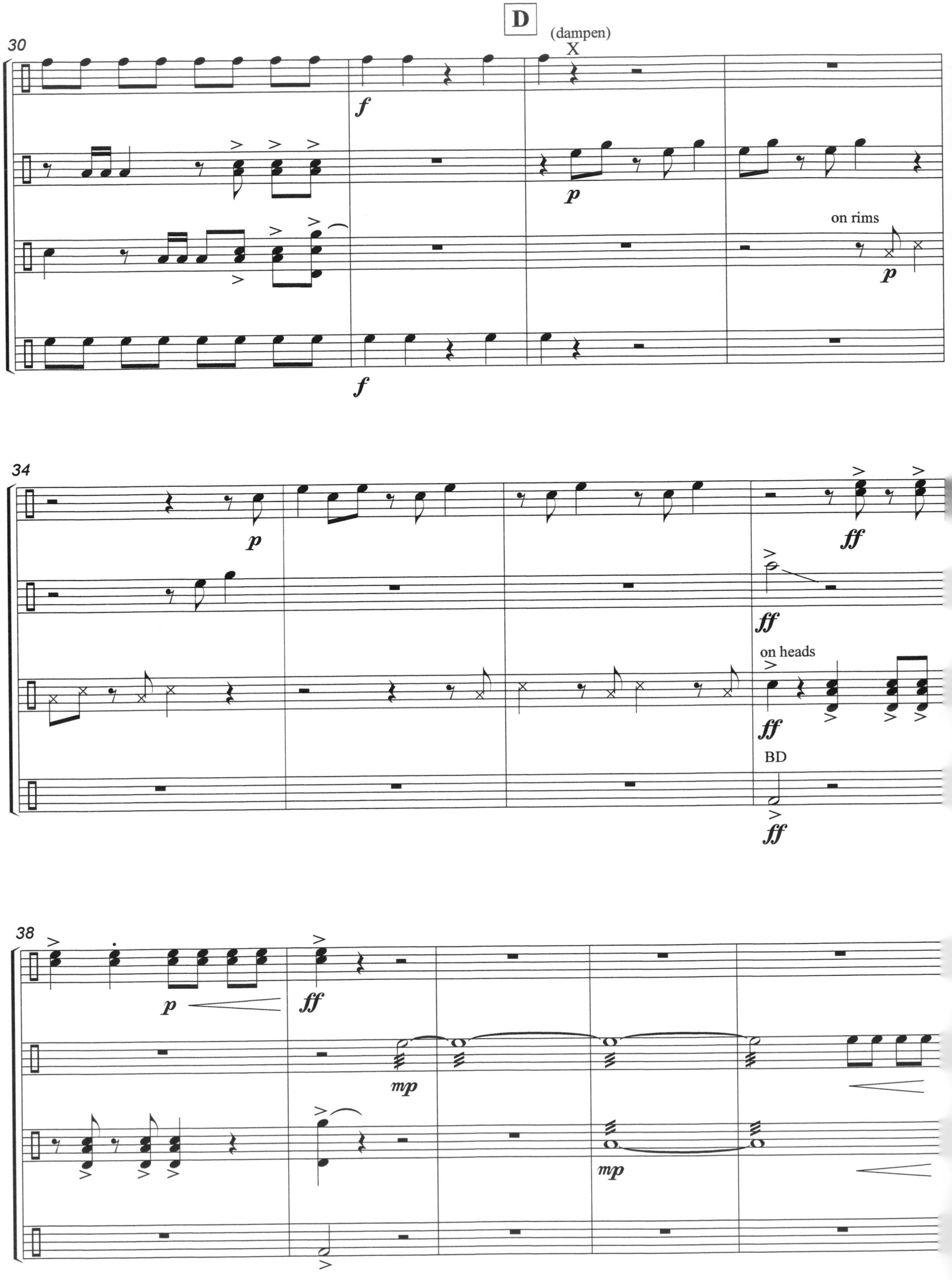
D
(dampen)
X
30
1
2
3
4
f
p
f
on rims
p
34
p
ff
ff
on heads
ff
BD
ff
38
p
ff
mp
mp

- denotes a weighty stress. All *tenuto* notes create a compound melody throughout the ensemble during *Adagio* sections.

PERCUSSION 1:
2 Triangles, Cowbell,
Bongos

Written for and premiered by the Pittsburg State University Percussion Ensemble,
Directed by the Composer, May 6, 1997, McCray Hall, Pittsburg, Kansas

Elephant Breath

Evan Hause
(1997)

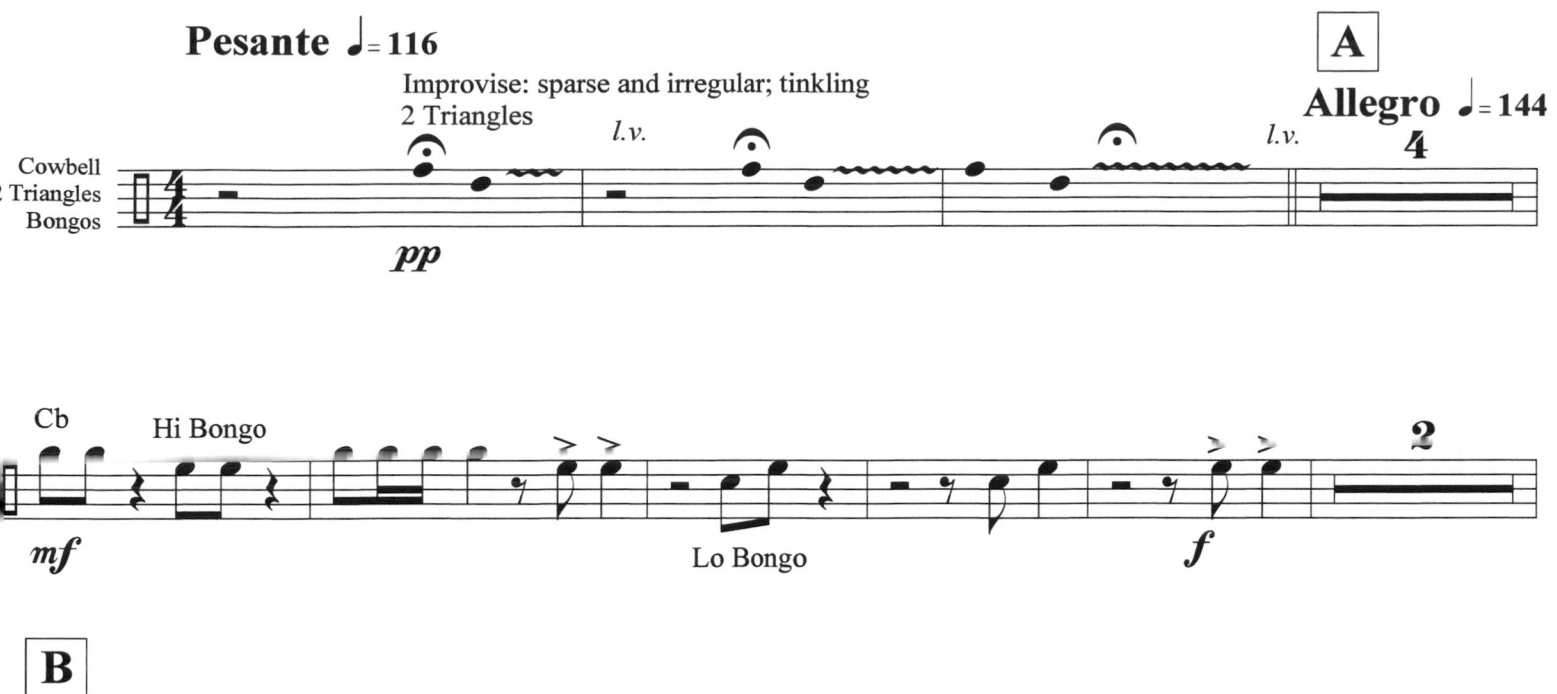

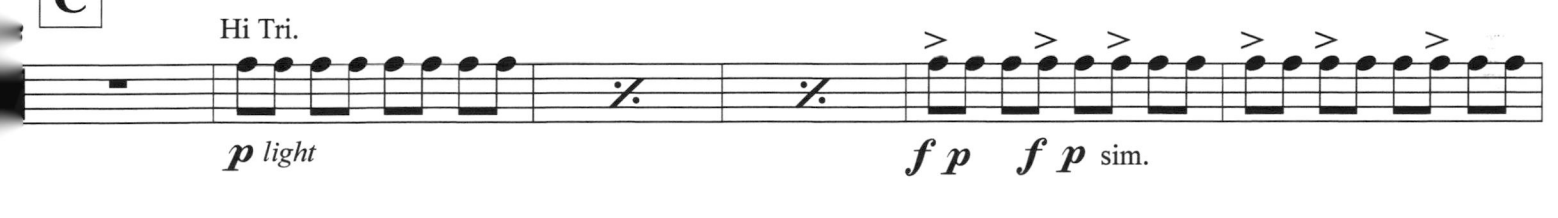

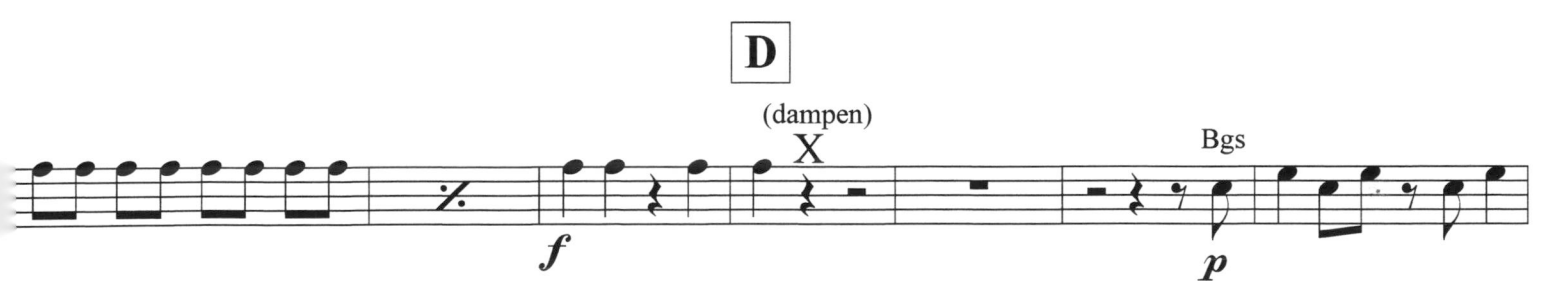

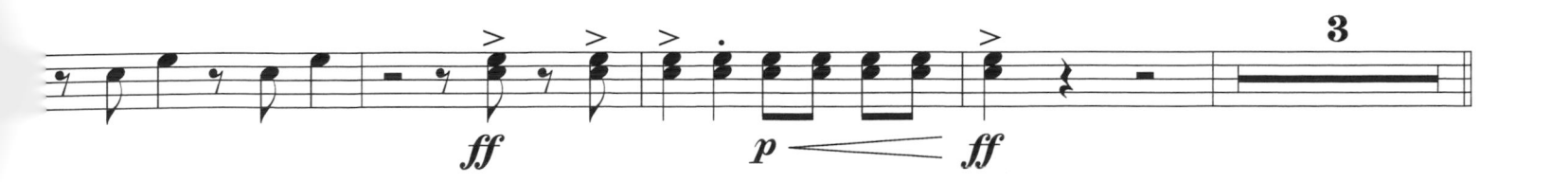

denotes a weighty stress. All *tenuto* notes create a compound melody throughout the ensemble
ing *Adagio* sections.

TURN and PLAY (fast)

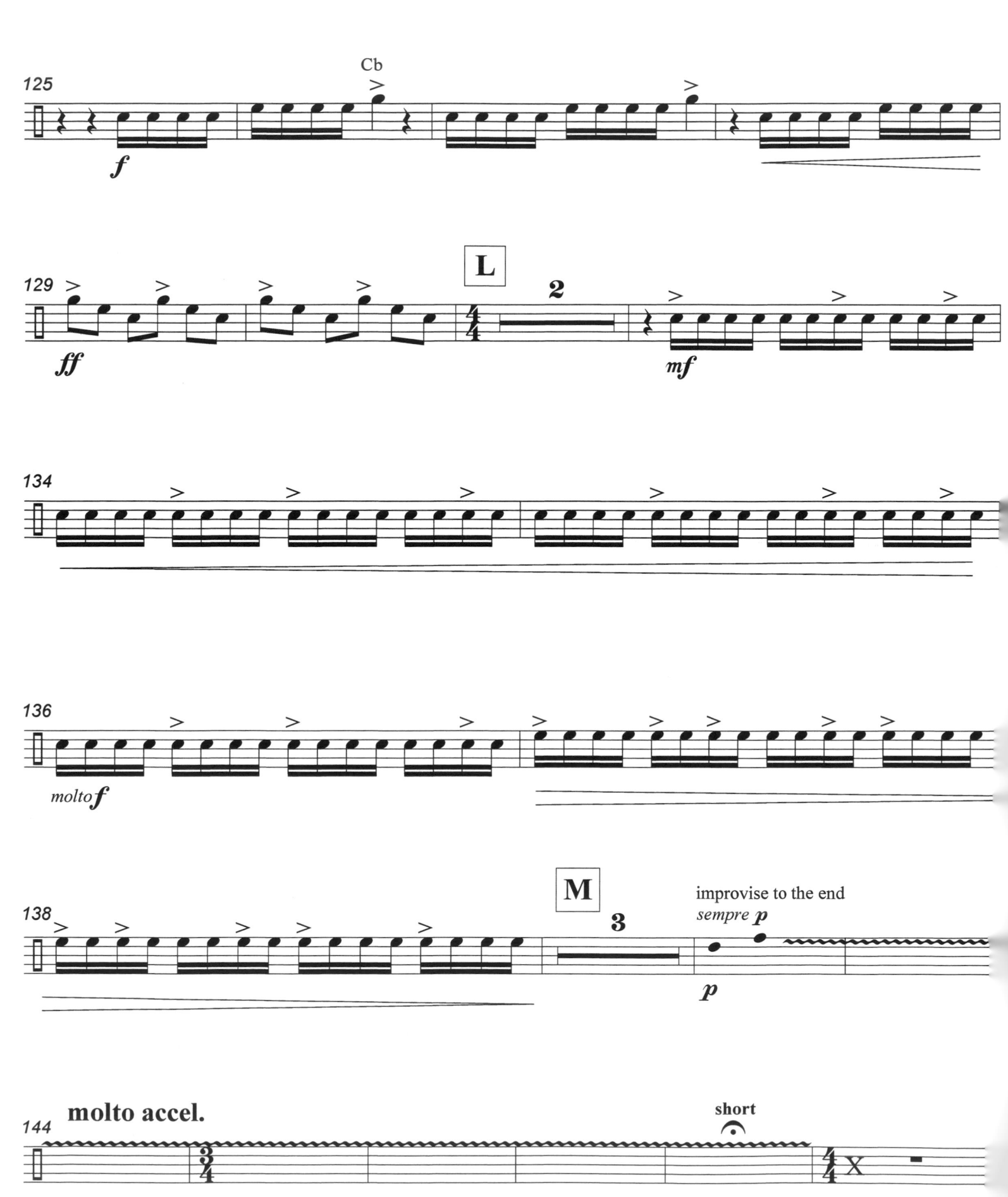

April 8, 199
Pittsburg, K

* – denotes a weighty stress. All *tenuto* notes create a compound melody throughout the ensemble during *Adagio* sections.

82
G
SB
f
2
88
H
f
92
I
mf
stick shots
p
f
J
2
MT
ff
mp
♩= 116
stop playing;
l.v.
SB
slow tremolo
Presto ♩= 164
f
Adagio (Tempo III)

April 8, 1997
Pittsburg, KS

April 8, 1997
Pittsburg, KS

TURN FAST

April 8, 1997
Pittsburg, KS

PERCUSSION 3

Written for and premiered by the Pittsburg State University Percussion Ensemble,
Directed by the Composer, May 6, 1997, McCray Hall, Pittsburg, Kansas

Quasi-drum kit:
Medium crash-ride Cymbal,
Kick Drum, Snare Drum,
Tenor Drum (or 16" Tom-tom)

Elephant Breath

Evan Hause
(1997)

TURN and PLAY

* – denotes a weighty stress. All *tenuto* notes create a compound melody throughout the ensemble during *Adagio* sections.

PERCUSSION 4:
Concert Bass Drum
Tambourine
China Cymbal

Written for and premiered by the Pittsburg State University Percussion Ensemble,
Directed by the Composer, May 6, 1997, McCray Hall, Pittsburg, Kansas

Elephant Breath

Evan Hause
(1997)

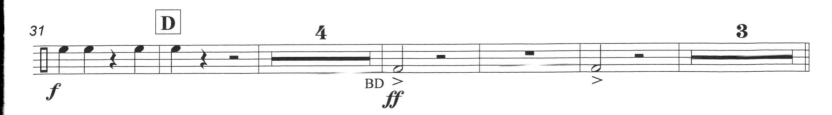

* – denotes a weighty stress. All *tenuto* notes create a compound melody throughout the ensemble during *Adagio* sections.

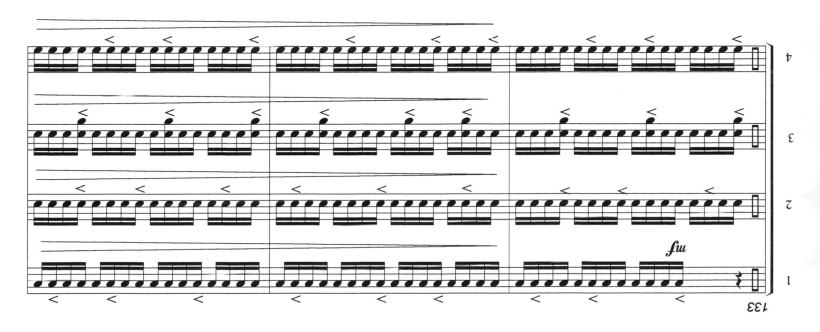

April 8, 1997
Pittsburg, KS